TWELVE SONS
of
BRITAIN

TWELVE SONS
of
BRITAIN

General Authorities Born in England

by Lawrence R. Flake

CFI
Springville, Utah

ISBN 13: 978-1-59955-136-4

Published by CFI, an imprint of Cedar Fort, Inc., 2373 W. 700 S., Springville, UT, 84663
Distributed by Cedar Fort, Inc. www.cedarfort.com

LIBRARY OF CONGRESS CATALOGING-IN-PUBLICATION DATA

Flake, Lawrence R. (Lawrence Read).
    Twelve sons of Britain : general authorities of the Church of Jesus Christ of Latter-day Saints who were born in England / Lawrence Flake.
        p. cm.
    ISBN 978-1-59955-136-4
    1. Mormons—England—Biography. 2. Mormons—United States—Biography. 3. Church of Jesus Christ of Latter-day Saints—Biography. I. Title.
    BX8693.F59 2008
    289.3092'242—dc22
    [B]
                            2007052170

Cover design by Jeremy Beal
Cover design © 2008 by Lyle Mortimer
Edited and typeset by Lyndsee Simpson Cordes

Printed in the United States of America

10 9 8 7 6 5 4 3 2 1

Printed on acid-free paper

This book is dedicated to my noble English ancestors,
the Flakes and the Reads.

———————————

I also express appreciation to William W. Slaughter
and Ronald Read of the Church History Department and
to Richard Nietzel Holzapfel of the BYU Religious Studies
Center for providing the photographs for this book.

TABLE OF CONTENTS

INTRODUCTION

It would be difficult to overstate the contributions of England to the restored kingdom of God on the earth. President Gordon B. Hinckley made reference to some of these great gifts to the world and the Church from this island nation in his dedicatory prayer for England's second temple in 1998. "Through the centuries Thou hast smiled with favor upon England, 'this sceptered isle.' Great have been her ways, marvelous her destiny. She has bequeathed to the world the great principles of English law to enhance the dignity of man, and the priceless gift of the English Bible which since the year 1611 has stood as a testament of the Redeemer of the world."[1]

When the Prophet Joseph Smith sent two apostles and five other missionaries to England in 1837, they found a people prepared by the Spirit of the Lord, and thousands were baptized. When one of the apostles, Heber C. Kimball, told Joseph Smith of the great spirit they found there, the Prophet declared "the reason he felt as he did in the streets of Chatburn was because the place was indeed 'holy ground,' that some of the ancient prophets had traveled in that region and dedicated the land, and that he, Elder Kimball, had reaped the benefit of their blessing."[2] Five years later the Prophet sent seven more apostles as missionaries to the British Isles, and the harvest of souls was even greater, so much so that during the decade of the 1850s there were many more Latter-day Saints in England than in the United States.

Over the next thirty years, most of these faithful English members immigrated to Utah and became the stalwart forebears of generations of Latter-day Saints. This fact was powerfully demonstrated in 1982 when the Tabernacle Choir sang in London's prestigious Royal Albert Hall. At the conclusion of the concert, the announcer requested that all those among the 375 voice choir who were descendants of British converts please stand. All but six of the singers arose!

No nation except the United States has made a greater contribution to the leadership of the Church than has Great Britain. The most important Mormon born in England was of course John Taylor, third president of the Church. He is followed closely by his convert and nephew George Q. Cannon, who served as a counselor to four presidents of the Church and would likely have become president himself had he lived six months longer. Four other native born Englishmen, John R. Winder, Charles Penrose, George Teasdale, and James E. Talmage also became apostles. Elders Winder and Penrose likewise served in the First Presidency.

Two other deceased General Authorities born in England, Brigham H. Roberts and George Reynolds, were members of the First Council of the Seventy. Derek Cuthbert seved in the First Quorum of the Seventy until his death in 1991. Kenneth Johnson, the only living Briton among the Brethren, is presently serving as a member of that Quorum. John R. Winder was a counselor in the presiding bishopric, and John Longden was an assistant to the Quorum of the Twelve.

It is significant to note that two of these twelve men, James E. Talmage and B. H. Roberts, are listed among Mormonism's most important theologians. Elder Roberts also qualifies as one of the foremost Church historians of this dispensation.

What follows is a look at the lives of each of these remarkable "Twelve sons of Britain" in the chronological order of their birth, beginning with their roots in England.

Notes

1. " 'Thou Hast Smiled . . . Upon England,' " *Church News*, June 13, 1998, 4.
2. Orson F. Whitney, *Life of Heber C. Kimball* (Salt Lake City: Bookcraft, 1974), 188.

John Taylor

Birth: 1 November 1808, Milnthorpe, Westmoreland County, England

Baptism: 9 May 1836

Emigrated: 1831

Ordination to the Quorum of the Twelve: 19 December 1838

Ordination as President of the Quorum of the Twelve: 6 October 1877

Ordination as President of the Church: 10 October 1880

Death: 25 July 1887 (age 78), Kaysville, Utah

The Lake District in Northern England is known for being one of the loveliest regions in the country. Its fertile green fields, flowering hillsides, rolling mountains, and sparkling lakes were the setting that inspired nature-loving writers such as William Wordsworth, Samuel Coleridge, Percy Bysshe Shelley, and other romantic poets to compose their poems of lyric beauty. It was in this pastoral area that John Taylor entered mortality. He was the only President of the Church to be born outside the United States.

As a young man, his father, James Taylor, inherited several pieces of property, including a house in the town of Milnthorpe. James married a woman of the same surname, Agnes Taylor, though they were not related. They first lived in Burton, Westmoreland, where their first son, Edward, was born. By 1808 the Taylors had moved to James's inherited property in Milnthorpe, where John, their second son and the future apostle and prophet, was born on 1 November 1808. A house still stands on what is now called Bridge End Farm at Stainton, Westmoreland County (now Cumbria County), which is believed to be his birthplace.[1]

In 1814, following the birth of three more sons, the Taylor family moved to Liverpool, south of Hale, where they lived for about five years. Little is known about their time there; James worked for the Excise, a tax department of the British government. Upon their return to the Lake District, four more children joined the Taylor family, making nine in all. The Taylors settled in Hale, a few miles south of Milnthorpe, on another of the properties James had inherited. The Church has placed a historic marker in front of the house on this farm in honor of President Taylor.

The Taylors' sons worked hard on the farm, helping with the orchards, animals, bees, and crops. President Taylor later wrote, "In this place I got mixed up with ploughing, sowing, reaping, haymaking, and so forth, and have indelibly impressed on my mind some of my first mishaps in horsemanship in the shape of sundry curious evolutions between the horses' backs and *terra firma*."[2]

Besides working on his parents' farm, John attended school at Beetham, one mile from their home in Hale. As was the custom of the time, at age fourteen his labors at farming were exchanged for a stint as an apprentice. John went to work with a barrel maker in Liverpool. After a year, the business failed, and John was subsequently apprenticed to a wood turner in Penrith, north of Hale in the Lake District, where he remained for five years.

All accounts of President Taylor's formative years, including his own writings, describe him as a religious boy. His parents were active and committed members of the Anglican Church; they paid their tithing and made sure that their children learned their catechism and said their prayers. John was christened and given godparents in Heversham parish near their home in Milnthorpe. President Taylor recalled that when he was still a boy, he saw "an angel in the heavens holding a trumpet to his mouth."[3] This was the first of many spiritual manifestations that eventually led him to embrace the restored gospel.[4]

Feeling that something was missing from the Anglican Church, John became impressed with the preaching of the Methodists and affiliated himself with this movement at age seventeen. He became what was called "an exhorter," or, more simply said, a lay preacher. In the company of another young member of his new faith, while walking near the town of Penrith a few miles from where they had been assigned to preach, John stopped suddenly and expressed a strong impression he had that he must go to America to preach. He considered this a revelatory and prophetic prompting, which he never forgot and which his future as a missionary and apostle in the restored church fully fulfilled. Many other strong spiritual experiences followed. He wrote, "I had frequent manifestations in dreams, and otherwise frequently when alone, and sometimes in company, I heard sweet soft melodious music, as if performed by angelic or supernatural beings."[5]

During these years in the beautiful Lake District, he spent

most of his spare time either reading religious works or praying. He wrote, "Most of my leisure hours were spent in reading the Bible, works on theology and in prayer. . . . I went into secluded places in the fields and woods, in barns and other secret places. I also got together boys of the same age to join with me in secret prayer; but they generally soon forsook me."[6] The fact that he alone persisted among his peers is reason to surmise that his religious fervor was unusual.

In 1828, at the age of twenty, he returned to Hale and began working in the carpenter trade, but not for long. Two years later his family decided to immigrate to the New World. They had recently lost their oldest son, Edward, to an untimely death, so John, now the oldest, was left behind in England to sell the farm. He crossed the ocean alone several months later to join his family in America.

A severe storm at sea during his journey caused great distress and fear among the ship's passengers and crew but did not trouble him, for his strong conviction that he would live to preach in America made him bold in the face of it. "So confident was I of my destiny that I went on deck at midnight, and amidst the raging elements felt as calm as though I was sitting in a parlor at home. I believed I should reach America and perform my work."[7] After spending a few weeks in New York, he continued on to Toronto, where his family had settled. There he began his own business as a carpenter.

In Toronto he continued his interest in Methodism and began studying with a group of people who were interested in the primitive church of Jesus Christ and had observed how much the churches of their day had diverged from the New Testament church. Within his acquaintances at church, he met and proposed marriage to Leonora Cannon (a sister of George Q. Cannon's father). At first she declined his proposal—probably because she was ten years his senior—but following a dream in which she saw herself happily in his company, she accepted.

Some months earlier, in Kirtland, Ohio, Heber C. Kimball

had given his fellow apostle, Parley P. Pratt, a blessing and had prophesied that he would go to Toronto. Elder Kimball said, "And there thou shalt find a people prepared for the fullness of the gospel, and they shall receive thee, and many shall be brought to the knowledge of the truth and shall be filled with joy; and from the things growing out of this mission, shall the fullness of the gospel spread into England, and cause a great work to be done in that land."[8] Shortly after his arrival in Toronto, Elder Pratt found the Taylors, and John found the compelling truth for which he had been searching all his life. His motto became, "The kingdom of God or nothing." He and Leonora were baptized along with many members of their study group on 9 May 1836. Soon after his baptism, John was given charge of all the affairs of the Church in Canada.

In 1837 he journeyed to Kirtland, arriving in the midst of the huge controversy over the failure of the Kirtland Safety Society. Many members and even leaders were apostatizing. To his great consternation, he found Parley P. Pratt, the missionary who brought him into the gospel, wavering in his faith. He confronted him with his own powerful testimony, admonishing Elder Pratt, "Now Brother Parley, it is not man that I am following, but the Lord. The principles you taught me led me to Him, and I now have the same testimony that you then rejoiced in. If the word was true six months ago, it is true today; if Joseph Smith was then a prophet, he is now a prophet."[9] The powerful words and conviction of his convert softened Parley's heart; he repented and recommitted himself to the gospel. He never wavered again and died a martyr's death while serving a mission in 1857. Elder Taylor returned to Canada for a time but soon took his family and cast his lot with the Saints in Missouri, suffering all the persecution and turmoil they were forced to endure. In 1838, when John Boynton abandoned his position as one of the Twelve, the Lord called John Taylor to fill the vacancy. Brigham Young ordained him an apostle at a conference in Far West on 5 October 1838.

When the Saints were expelled from Missouri in 1838,

Elder Taylor established his family in a poor shelter on the Montrose side of the Mississippi River across from what would become Nauvoo. In 1839 Elder Taylor left them in near desperate circumstances in order to return in secret with other apostles to Far West, Missouri. The Prophet Joseph Smith had prophesied earlier that the apostles would leave from that place to fulfill a great mission in England. Elder Taylor was headed back to preach in his native land.

He had many hardships along the way, being ill and not having money for his passage, but the Lord blessed him with people who helped and strengthened him. Arriving in Liverpool, the first house he visited was the home of his wife's brother George Cannon. The family was converted, including their twelve-year-old son, George Q. Cannon, whose importance in the future of the Church is legendary. The mission of the apostles in England was a remarkable success, laying the foundation for all that would follow. John Taylor made a monumental contribution by helping to publish the Book of Mormon and other much-needed Church materials in England.

John Taylor and Joseph Smith were fast friends. Elder Taylor stood by the Prophet through thick and thin, constantly testifying of Joseph's prophetic calling and noble character. Voluntarily joining Joseph and Hyrum when they were incarcerated in Carthage Jail, John Taylor was present at their martyrdom. Shortly before the fatal shootings, at the Prophet's request, John sang "A Poor Wayfaring Man of Grief," which he described as a plaintive, pathetic song. He said, "[It] was very much in accordance with our feelings at the time for our spirits were all depressed, dull and gloomy and surcharged with indefinite ominous forebodings."[10] When the mob attacked, John Taylor was shot four times but was preserved from a fatal wound to the heart by a pocket watch, which repelled the bullet. Following the death of the Prophet, he wrote a letter to Nauvoo urging the Saints not to commit violence in reaction to the outrage. He also authored the eulogy that became section

135 of the Doctrine and Covenants, chronicling the events of the tragedy for posterity and penning the now-famous lines, "Joseph Smith, the Prophet and Seer of the Lord, has done more, save Jesus only, for the salvation of men in this world, than any other man that ever lived in it" (D&C 135:3).

In subsequent years he continued to serve important missions for the Church—a second mission to England from 1846 to 1847; a mission to Europe from 1848 to 1852, where he opened the work in France; and a mission to the Eastern States from 1855 to 1857. During this last mission, he became a powerful advocate for Mormonism through a newspaper called the *Mormon*, which he published in New York City. He knew many influential people and made some valiant efforts to move Utah toward statehood but was thwarted by the anti-polygamy sentiment, which had begun to rage, and which plagued the Church for the rest of John Taylor's life.

In 1857, the First Presidency called him home from the East, along with the rest of the missionaries of the Church, because of the threat of Johnston's army moving toward Utah. Established again in Utah, he became a powerful advocate for the Church and for the right of the Saints to practice their religion, including polygamy. He was known by several titles throughout his life—Champion of Truth, Champion of Right, Champion of Liberty. Whatever else he may have been, he was certainly a champion. He served in the Utah legislature from 1857 to 1870, acting as Speaker of the House for most of those sessions. He also served as a probate judge in Utah County. During the fight against government intervention in polygamy, he always advocated avoiding violent conflicts and not retaliating but calmly standing firm for freedom of religion and legal negotiation to arrive at the desired ends.

Upon Brigham Young's death in 1877, John Taylor, the senior member of the Twelve, assumed leadership of the Quorum. For three years, no new president was sustained. The Quorum of the Twelve, with Elder Taylor as president, presided over the Church in what was called an apostolic interregnum.

In 1880 the new First Presidency was formed with John Taylor as president of the Church and George Q. Cannon and Joseph F. Smith as counselors.

By this time, many faithful members of the Church, including President Taylor, had entered into the practice of polygamy. During his presidency, many brethren were imprisoned for following this practice. It was President Taylor who, upon visiting the Arizona Saints and seeing the impossibility of their plight, advised them to move to Mexico to avoid the harsh imprisonments and raids they were suffering. In 1885, pursued by government officials himself, President Taylor went into hiding. He dared not even attend the funeral of one of his wives, Sophia. He endured the bitter hardship of exile for two years and then succumbed to heart failure, dying on 25 July 1887 at the age of seventy-nine. Many said he would assuredly have lived longer had he been allowed to remain in the company of his loved ones, which consisted of a family of seven wives and thirty-five children.[11]

Even though suffering this severe persecution, President Taylor managed to lead the Church through a period of growth, endurance, and success. In 1878, under his leadership, the Primary organization was established. In 1880 he proclaimed a Jubilee Year, fashioned after the Old Testament tradition, and urged members of the Church to follow the ancient practice of forgiving debts. Work on the Salt Lake and Manti Temples continued under his leadership along with the completion of the Logan Temple and its dedication on 17 May 1884. He established the practice of financial support for full-time Church leaders, who were too busy to manage their own business affairs. He promoted charitable works and was ever an engaging and powerful speaker. He was said to have been twice a martyr—once in Carthage jail and again as he died in exile for the cause he had so valiantly defended all his life.

From an obscure English boy, a mere wood turner, John Taylor rose to fulfill the prophetic calling he felt so deeply as a young man. He truly answered the call to preach in America and truly earned the titles he was known by: "Champion of Truth, Right, and Liberty."

Notes
1. Jack E. Jarrard, "John Taylor Home Photos Show Typical English Farm," *Church News*, 8 Dec. 1973, 5.
2. John Taylor, "History of John Taylor by Himself," photocopy, in Manuscript History of the Church, book G, 265, Archives Division, The Church of Jesus Christ of Latter-day Saints, Salt Lake City, Utah; in Paul Thomas Smith, "Young John Taylor," *Ensign*, Jun. 1993, 8.
3. Ibid., 266–67; in Smith, 9.
4. Ibid., 265–67; in Smith, 8–9.
5. Ibid., 266–67; in Smith, 9.
6. Ibid., 265–67; in Smith, 8–9.
7. B. H. Roberts, *Life of John Taylor* (Salt Lake City: Bookcraft, 1994), 29.
8. Larry C. Porter, "Parley P. Pratt's Canada Mission Opened Door for Proselyting in British Isles," *Church News*, 14 Dec. 1986, 7.
9. Roberts, *Life*, 40.
10. B. H. Roberts, *History of the Church* (Salt Lake City: Deseret News, 1957), 7:101.
11. Daniel H. Ludlow, ed., *Encyclopedia of Mormonism* (New York: Macmillan Publishing, 1992), 4:1440.

JOHN REX WINDER

Birth: 11 December 1821, Biddenham, Kent County, England
Baptism: 20 September 1848
Emigration: 1853
Ordination as Second Counselor to Presiding Bishop William Bowker Preston: 8 April 1887
Ordination as First Counselor to President Joseph F. Smith: 17 October 1901
Death: 27 March 1910 (Age 88), Salt Lake City, Utah

The small English village of Biddenham in Kent County had been the home of the Winder family for generations when, on 11 December 1821, John Rex Winder was born. He was named for an older brother who had died just two years before. With his siblings, John was taught to read and write, to work hard on the family farm, and to trust in God. Recalling his youth, he wrote,

> I was sent out into the fields to keep the birds off the grain, and it was a very lonely spot, surrounded with woods. Being entirely alone, I was somewhat fearful, and I remember that I was impressed to kneel down in the brush to pray to the Lord that His angels might watch over and protect me from harm. I remember now just as well as I see your faces, that that was the end of my fear. I also think that that was the beginning of my success in life. Although that spot is many thousand miles distant, and it is more than seventy years ago, I could walk straight to that very spot where I knelt down, and where I received that blessing.[1]

The blessing and guidance of the Lord that John received as a boy stayed with him as he grew and led him to his eternal companion and The Church of Jesus Christ of Latter-day Saints. He found both of these blessings at age twenty, when he traveled to the sprawling Victorian city of London to seek his fortune. Taking a position at the West End Shoe and Grocery Store, John began to develop his skills as a leather worker. One day he noticed some small scraps of paper on the floor of the shop. He recalled, "A person had torn up a letter into very small fragments and thrown it on the floor. I was impressed to pick up a small piece of it, and on that piece of paper were the two words 'Latter-day Saint.' I looked at it and wondered what it meant. I never had heard of Latter-day Saints, or Mormons, or Joseph Smith, or anything of the kind. I was impressed to take it over and ask the man who was at the desk what it meant."[2]

To his great surprise, the man at the desk was himself a Latter-day Saint and was not only able to tell him about this unpopular American religion, but even the location where the Mormons held their meetings. John determined to attend, but on his first visit, being rather shy by nature, he crept up the back stairs and peered through the banister. Elder Orson Spencer was preaching. "I thought he knew I was there," John said, "for every word he spoke fit my case and seemed to be for my express benefit."[3]

Very soon John and his new bride, Ellen Walters, whom he had also met at his place of employment, were both baptized—he on 20 September 1848 and she a few weeks later on 15 October 1848. The reason for this delay was that just one day before John's baptism, she had given birth to a son, John R. Winder Jr. Her baptism was performed by the apostle Orson Pratt. Like most converts of the time, the Winders began dreaming and planning to immigrate to America to join with the Saints in the Rocky Mountains. It took five years, but in February of 1853, they and their growing family were finally on their way, aboard the *Elvira Owen*. The family consisted of a four-year-old son, twin baby daughters, and a young Irish girl whom they had more or less adopted.

The journey across the Atlantic turned out to be a major ordeal for the whole family when, ten days out, John was stricken with small pox. The dreaded, highly contagious disease had been brought on board by an infected child who was staying next to the Winders on the ship. The plague was contained and limited to just five persons by immediately establishing quarantined quarters on board the boat. The crew built a small house on deck for the infected passengers. Of course Ellen was left to care for the family without John's aid. Brother Winder said, "To add to our anxiety, one of the patients, lying next to me, a young brother named William Jones, died a few days later, about nine o'clock in the evening, and soon the sailors came and took the body out and cast it into the sea. I heard them say, 'We will have him next,' meaning me, but I had faith that I would recover and get to Zion, and in due time my faith was confirmed."[4]

Plying his skill with leather in Salt Lake City, John began making boots and saddles and later went into the tanning business with several partners, including President Brigham Young. As a captain in the Utah Nauvoo Legion, John and fifty militia men were among the units assigned to guard Echo Canyon against the U.S. Army during the fall and winter of 1857–58. Distinguishing himself in various military expeditions, including the Blackhawk War, Brother Winder earned the rank of lieutenant colonel. In addition to holding more than twenty prominent governmental and business positions, Brother Winder presided as patriarch over a large family of four wives and twenty children.

At the age of sixty-five, Elder Winder was called as a counselor to Presiding Bishop William B. Preston. In 1892, while he was serving in this position, President Woodruff set a goal to finish the construction of the Salt Lake Temple by the next April, making the building time forty years from start to finish. Bishop Winder was given the responsibility for seeing that the 250-man crew met this deadline. After the dedication on 6 April 1893, he was called as first assistant to the temple president, Lorenzo Snow. In 1901, just two months short of his eightieth birthday, he was called to serve as first counselor in the First Presidency of the Church under President Joseph F. Smith. His reaction to this call shows his characteristic humility: "To think that one who had sprung from the source I had, without any education . . . slow to speech, feeling as though I could pass through the floor whenever I am called upon to speak to the people—was it possible that President Smith could choose me for his counselor?"[5]

At the time of Brother Winder's death nine years later, President Smith gave this evaluation: "If any man loved him any more than I do, I say God bless that man. In his military career and all other phases of his life, he never sought office nor honors; they were always in search of him. Heaven itself could scarcely be more true than President Winder was true."[6]

Notes

1. Michael K. Winder, *Counselors to the Prophets* (Roy, UT: Eborn Books, 2001), 49–50.
2. Ibid.
3. Orson F. Whitney, *History of Utah* (Salt Lake City: George Q. Cannon, & Sons, 1892), 4:240, s.v. "John Rex Winder."
4. Winder, 251.
5. Edward H. Anderson, "President John R. Winder," *Improvement Era*, May 1910, 626.
6. Ibid.

GEORGE QUAYLE CANNON

Birth: 11 January 1827, Liverpool, Lancashire County, England

Baptism: 18 June 1840

Emigration: 1842

Ordination to the Quorum of the Twelve: 26 August 1860

Ordination as Additional Counselor to President Brigham Young: 8 April 1873

Ordination as Assistant Counselor to President Brigham Young: 9 May 1874

Returned to the Quorum of the Twelve: 29 August 1877

Ordination as First Counselor to President John Taylor: 10 October 1880

Returned to the Quorum of the Twelve: 25 July 1887

Ordination as First Counselor to President Wilford Woodruff: 7 April 1889

Ordination as First Counselor to President Lorenzo Snow: 13 September 1898

Death: 12 April 1901 (age 74), Monterey, California

George Quayle Cannon was born 11 January 1827 in Liverpool, England, the eldest of seven children.[1] His parents, George Cannon and Ann Quayle Cannon, were both from the Isle of Man. His interest in religion began early. As an adult, he remembered the sorrow he felt as a very young child because he did not live in New Testament times. He wrote, "I have wept because I did not live on the earth when Jesus wandered among men. And I have asked myself, why it is that men cannot receive those blessings as they who were the associates of Jesus received them? I asked my teachers, and I asked my parents, 'Are there men now who receive these blessings?' and they answered me that there were none, and I wondered why it was so."[2] He also recalled, "I can remember in my early boyhood that I felt very badly because I had no especial gift, and I used to think I was not a favored child of God, else I would have received the gift of tongues or some other such gift."[3]

The story of George Q. Cannon's conversion begins with his father's sister, Leonora Cannon, who immigrated to Canada and married John Taylor. When John Taylor went on the first apostolic missionary journey to England, in 1839, the Cannon home at 43 Norfolk Street in Liverpool was the first one he visited. To the great joy of Leonora, her beloved brother and his wife accepted the message of the restored gospel from her husband. At first only the parents were baptized. But even at age thirteen, their young son George had a compelling interest in the discussion of Mormonism. He wrote, "We had many people come to our house to talk about [the gospel]. I was sent to bed with my brother David, the baby, but I would get up when he was asleep and sit on the stairs and listen to them converse on the gospel. My father found me asleep, and said I must be allowed to sit up or I would fall and break my neck."[4]

Eventually it dawned on the missionaries that several of the Cannon children were old enough to be baptized. George, age thirteen, and Mary Alice, age eleven, received permission. The Cannon parents thought their little sister Ann, just barely eight years old, was too young to make such a commitment, but she "wept so bitterly at being left out that she was also allowed to join them, and the three were baptized into The Church of Jesus Christ of Latter-day Saints."[5] Now George knew where he could find the blessings of the New Testament on the earth and how he could obtain his "especial gift."

At the time of the family's conversion, George was still in school. He was an apt student, having learned his letters and how to read at age four. He also excelled in math and penmanship. He recalled an incident at school that again demonstrates his deep religious feelings:

> When I was a little boy about twelve years of age, I was asked in school what I would like to be. The boys were talking about their future occupations—they knew I was a Mormon and I remarked that I wanted to be an elder in The Church of Jesus Christ of Latter-day Saints. That was my highest ambition; that was my strongest desire; it was that I might preach this Gospel, that I would like to spend my days in preaching the Gospel. I was very young, but I did love the Gospel; I loved the truth, and I sought to obtain a knowledge concerning it, and the Lord granted that request to me, and when He granted it to me, I was perfectly happy.[6]

After their conversion, the Cannon family, in keeping with the doctrine of their day, greatly desired to immigrate to Nauvoo and join with the Saints in Zion. George's mother had prudently saved a secret fund from her household allowances and pledged to use this money for their passages. Young George wanted to contribute to the finances as well and begged to be allowed to quit school and work for wages. His parents at first denied this request, but so persistent was he, that they finally allowed him to do so. Upon leaving school he was awarded a fine Bible for good behavior, a tribute to his excellence as a student. His first job was with the Liverpool and Manchester Railroad. He worked in the shipping office, and it was said that his job enabled him to hone his handwriting until it "came to look like copper plate engraving."[7] His employer at the shipping office paid another tribute to young George's talent by asking him to stay behind in England and live with his family. He "promised to make him an expert and master of the newly born and stupendous problems of transportation."[8] But George's desire to serve the Lord vastly outweighed any career ambitions, and so when the Cannons departed on 17 September 1842 aboard the *Sidney* bound for St. Louis, George was aboard. The voyage proved to be a tragic one for the Cannons. Sister Cannon, who was pregnant and who had long had a premonition that she would die on the ocean, succumbed and was buried at sea. Brother Cannon expressed his deep sorrow, longing to join her: "Although in expectation of bearing many things which are not of a pleasant nature—privation or poverty we agreed to share with the Saints, but we are tried in a more tender part, and were it not for our helpless children's sake I should like to repose under the peaceful blue waters with her who shared my every joy and sorrow. Heavenly Father keep me from repining! But seeing other people enjoying the society of those they love, my heart sickens and I long to be at rest with my dear wife."[9]

And so, George Q. Cannon, age fifteen, and his five little brothers and sisters were left motherless in the middle of the ocean, heading for a strange new land.

After wintering in St. Louis, the little Cannon clan journeyed on to Nauvoo. It happened that a conference was in session there, so many of the Saints had gathered on the pier to meet the boat. On arriving in America, young George had another spiritual experience, which he remembered all of his life. Upon seeing the Prophet Joseph Smith amid the crowd of spectators, without having anyone point him out, George picked him out instantly. He wrote, "[I] would haven know him among ten thousand. There was that about him which to [my] eyes, distinguished him from all the men [I] had ever seen."[10]

George worked at his uncle Elder John Taylor's printing establishment, where two newspapers were published, the *Times and Seasons* and the *Nauvoo Neighbor*. A little more than a year later, the Cannons, along with all of Nauvoo, mourned the loss of their dear Prophet and his brother Hyrum. George's father, an accomplished carpenter and joiner, made the coffins and the death masks for the two fallen leaders. George was present at the meeting a few weeks later in which Sidney Rigdon campaigned for the leadership of the Church, and George witnessed the miracle that came to be known as the transfiguration of Brigham Young. He left this eyewitness account: "If Joseph had risen from the dead and again spoken in their hearing, the effect could not have been more startling than it was to many present at that meeting. It was the voice of Joseph himself, and not only was it the voice of Joseph which was heard; but it seemed in the eyes of the people as though it was the very person of Joseph which stood before them."[11]

In these troubled times following the Prophet's death, George's father was forced to travel to St. Louis to find decent employment, but sadly, quite suddenly and mysteriously, died there.[12] George and his sister Ann, now orphans, moved in with the Taylors, and George regarded his uncle as his surrogate father for the rest of his life.

On 16 February 1846, George assisted the Taylors in joining the forced mass exodus of the Saints from their beautiful city of Nauvoo to a crude camp on the Iowa side of the river. From here, enduring much hardship, he trekked on to the Salt Lake Valley with the second large company of the Saints, arriving on 5 October 1847. It was on this journey that he met his future wife, Elizabeth Hoagland, and established a firm friendship with her, which endured for many years until they were able to marry.

George Cannon remained in the valley for two years, helping his uncle establish a sawmill, planting crops, and battling crickets and hunger. In 1849 President Brigham Young called him to join a group of missionaries and travel to California to obtain much-needed funds for the Church by digging for gold.

A few months later, he set sail to Hawaii from San Francisco to fill the second of five successive missions. With the exception of nine months when he was not serving, his missions lasted over a period of fifteen years.[13]

After a five-year absence, Elder Cannon returned to Salt Lake Valley and married his sweetheart, Elizabeth Hoagland. Shortly after their marriage, she accompanied him on his next mission to San Francisco, this time to print the Book of Mormon in Hawaiian and publish a newspaper defending Mormonism, the *Western Standard*. A few weeks after his return from this assignment, Brother Cannon was called to serve another mission—this time to the East, where he became the chief executive in the Church's mammoth emigration operation. It was during this eastern mission that he learned of his calling to the Quorum of the Twelve apostles. He was ordained an apostle upon his return to Salt Lake City on 26 August 1860. As an apostle, he served his fifth mission, this time to his homeland of Great Britain as president of the European Mission. Upon his return to Utah in 1864, he was private secretary to Brigham Young for three years.[14]

In the winter of 1864–65, he devoted his outstanding executive talent to the organization of the Sunday School, the far-reaching influence of which is incalculable. In connection with this endeavor, he began the publication of the *Juvenile Instructor*, a magazine for Sunday School children. He was also the editor of the *Deseret News*. During the period from 1867 to 1882, Elder Cannon was engaged in various political activities, including many trips to Washington, D.C., in pursuit of statehood for Utah. He also served five terms as Utah's unofficial representative to Congress. His political career ended in 1882 when the seat to which he was elected in the House of Representatives was denied him because of his acceptance and practice of plural marriage. Elder Cannon had the distinction of serving as a counselor to four presidents of the Church: Brigham Young (1873–77), John Taylor (1880–87), Wilford Woodruff (1889–98,) and Lorenzo Snow (1898–1901). He was the senior apostle and would likely have become President of the Church had he lived six months longer.[15]

During his many years in Utah he was extremely involved in just about every aspect of the development of the Church and the state. He held offices in and sat on the boards of numerous companies, institutions, and enterprises such ZCMI, the Union Pacific Railroad, the Utah Sugar Company, the Brigham Young Trust Company, Utah Power and Light, Zion's Savings Bank & Trust Company, the Bullion-Beck & Champion Mining Company, and many others. He also acted as executor of Brigham Young's estate, which took many years to administer.[16]

During the bitter persecution against the Church for the practice of polygamy, Elder Cannon was a prime target. He went into hiding, as did many of the leaders of the Church, and was eventually arrested and imprisoned for four months in the Utah Penitentiary. The difficulties the Church encountered during the decade before the 1890 Manifesto banning polygamy was issued were tense and devastating. And Elder Cannon was always in the middle of the controversy. Even after the Manifesto, many problems continued to plague the Saints, but the Church endured the storm. Men of honor, like President Cannon, continued to support their families. He had four wives and twenty-eight children.[17]

After fifty years of devoted service to the Church, President Cannon returned to the Hawaiian Islands, the site of his first proselytizing mission. During this trip he revealed to his traveling companion a sacred experience he'd had there as a young missionary. He never spoke of it publicly until near the end of his life. Bryant S. Hinckley writes,

> The men are few in the world's history who have been granted the glorious visitation given to George Q. Cannon in his young days on that far distant island. There he talked to the Lord as one man talks with another. Fifty years afterward when he visited the Islands, during their Jubilee Celebration, 1900, he was riding with Brother Wooley,

touring the Islands. When he reached a certain place, he asked to get out, and he went along into the garden where fifty years before, the God of Heaven appeared to him, then a lonely and humble missionary.[18]

Elder Cannon also referred to this experience in a powerful testimony of the Savior: "I know that Jesus lives, for I have seen him. I know that this is the Church of God and that it is founded on Jesus Christ, our Redeemer. I testify to you of these things as one who knows—as one of the apostles of the Lord Jesus Christ that can bear witness to you today in the presence of the Lord that he lives and that he will live, and come to reign on the earth."[19]

Not long after his return from the Islands, his health began to fail. He traveled to the West Coast in an effort to recuperate but died in Monterey on 12 April 1901. It is difficult underestimate how well known and respected Elder Cannon was both inside and outside the Church. Comments from around the world attested to his greatness. Perhaps the comments of two national newspapers give some idea of how he was regarded outside Utah. The *Boston Globe* stated, "The death of George Q. Cannon removes from the sphere of worldly activities a Mormon leader who was second in power and influence only to that born ruler, Brigham Young himself."[20] The *San Francisco Examiner* gave him even a more superlative accolade: "George Q. Cannon, one of the most widely known men in America, banker, statesman, politician, missionary, railroad director, apostle and the recognized brains of the Mormon Church, is no more."[21]

Notes

1. Elder Cannon was named only George Cannon at birth, but he later added Quayle to his name to distinguish himself from another George Cannon he met in California in 1849 (*Church News*, 14 Jan. 1967).

2. E. L. Sloan, "Minutes of a Conference held in Bradford, Sunday, August 10, 1862," *Millennial Star* 22 (6 Sept. 1862): 563; in Lawrence R. Flake, *Prophets and Apostles of the Last Dispensation* (Provo, UT: Religious Studies Center, 2001), 181–82.

3. George Q. Cannon, "How I Obtained my Testimony of the Truth," *Young Women's Journal* 4 (Dec. 1892): 123; in Lawrence R. Flake, *George Q. Cannon: His Missionary Years* (Salt Lake City: Bookcraft, 1998), 14.
4. Beatrice Cannon Evans and Janath Russell Cannon, eds., *Cannon Family Historical Treasury* (Salt Lake City: Publishers Press, 1967), 161; in Flake, *Missionary Years*, 14.
5. Joseph J. Cannon, "George Q. Cannon," Instructor 79 (Feb. 1944): 73; in Flake, *Missionary Years*, 14.
6. George Q. Cannon, address to the Brigham Young Academy, Provo, Utah, Apr. 1889; in Flake, *Missionary Years*, 15.
7. Joseph J. Cannon, "George Q. Cannon," *Instructor* (Mar. 1944), 117; in Davis Bitton, *George Q. Cannon: A Biography* (Salt Lake City: Deseret Book Company, 1999), 38.
8. John Q. Cannon, *George Cannon: The Immigrant* (Salt Lake City, 1927), 145; in Flake, *Missionary Years*, 18.
9. Evans and Cannon, *Cannon Family*, 51; in Flake, *Missionary Years*, 18.
10. George Q. Cannon, "Early Experiences in Preaching," *Juvenile Instructor* (15 Feb. 1877), 48; in E. L. Sloan, *Prophets and Apostles*, 182.
11. George Q. Cannon letter, 28 Feb. 1861; in Flake, *Missionary Years*, 22.
12. George Q. Cannon letter, 24 Oct. 1863; in Flake, *Missionary Years*, 24
13. Some of the biographical profiles in this paper to a greater or lesser extent derive wording and ideas from vignettes I have previously written for two books I have authored, *Mighty Men of Zion* and *Prophets and Apostles of the Last Dispensation*, and entries I wrote for *LDS Encyclopedia of Church History*. See Lawrence R. Flake, s.v. "George Q. Cannon," in *LDS Encyclopedia of Church History*, eds. Arnold K. Garr et al. (Salt Lake City: Deseret Book Company, 2000), 181–82.
14. Ibid.
15. Ibid.
16. Ibid.
17. Ibid.
18. Bryant S. Hinckley, *Faith of Our Pioneer Fathers* (Salt Lake City: Deseret Book, 1965), 163; in Flake, *Missionary Years*, 213.
19. J. E. Cardon and Samuel O. Bennion, *Testimonies of the Divinity of the Church of Jesus Christ of Latter-day Saints* (Independence, MO: Zion's Publishing Company, 1930), 87.
20. *Boston Globe*, 13 Apr. 1901; in E. L. Sloan, *Prophets and Apostles*, 184.
21. *San Francisco Examiner*, 12 Apr. 1901; in E. L. Sloan, *Prophets and Apostles*, 2.

GEORGE TEASDALE

Birth: 8 December 1831, London, Middlesex County,
England
Baptism: 8 August 1852
Emigration: 1861
Ordination to the Quorum of the Twelve: 16 October
1882
Death: 9 June 1907 (age 75), Salt Lake City, Utah

On the morning of 13 October 1882, President John Taylor received a revelation in which the Lord called two worthy brethren to the Quorum of the Twelve apostles. President Taylor said, "Thus saith the Lord to the Twelve, and to the Priesthood and people of my Church: Let my servants George Teasdale and Heber J. Grant be appointed to fill the vacancies in the Twelve . . . for you have a great work to perform."[1] George Teasdale, age fifty at the time, had spent his thirty years since joining the Church in England serving the Lord with all his heart, might, mind, and strength. This call was the crowning one of many he had answered.

Elder Teasdale was born in London on 8 December 1831 to William Russell and Harriet Lidey Teasdale. He had a strong academic background after being educated in the English schools available to him in his day, including the University of London. After his basic education, he studied architecture, which enabled him to find employment with an architect in London, but, disillusioned with his dishonest employer, he began working in the upholstery trade.

His mother, a devout member of the Church of England, schooled George in their doctrines, but even though he was of a strongly spiritual nature, he did not find satisfaction in these tenets. He had studied the Bible on his own and was searching for something that rang more true to the teachings of the scriptures. In 1851, at the age of twenty, he came across an anti-Mormon tract, published by the Church of England. It made fascinating reading, and George was eager to learn more about the strange sect being attacked in the brochure. One day he discovered that one of his coworkers in the upholstery shop belonged to the new American religion. This man was not eloquent nor articulate in any way, but he bore such a powerful, humble testimony of his beliefs that George's heart was touched to the core. The other employees in the shop ridiculed both of them mercilessly, but neither was dissuaded, least of all George, "who became one of [Mormonism's] most ardent advocates."[2] He was baptized on 8 August 1852.

Although reticent and soft spoken by nature, he immediately began making a concerted effort to improve his speaking ability and soon joined with other early converts in doing missionary work. Though still required to make a living, he spent many hours in the ministry, serving as president of the Somerstown branch and clerk of the London Conference. While thus absorbed, he met and fell in love with a Latter-day Saint girl named Emily Emma Brown, who became his devoted wife, valiantly sharing many hardships with him throughout her life.[3]

In 1857, five years after his baptism, he was called to serve a full-time mission right there in his native land. He gave up his gainful employment, sold his home, situated his wife in more modest living circumstances, and devoted his entire energies to serving the Lord. His first assignment was as president of the Cambridge Conference, followed by service in the presidencies of several other areas within the large mission, which at that time included Scotland. Before the end of his mission in 1859, he was in charge of all the missionary work in Scotland.[4]

The Teasdales had long wished to follow the practice advocated by the leaders of the Church to immigrate to Zion as soon as possible. In their case, George's mission call detained them in England. When at last he was released, after serving as a full-time missionary for four years, they had very little money for their journey to Utah. Eventually, they managed to book places in steerage, the worst accommodations on the ship, the *Underwriter*, and began the long trip in 1861. It was no doubt a sad voyage, for they had buried two of their four children in England not long before their departure. Upon reaching the Salt Lake Valley, George found employment as a school teacher. Endowed with a pleasing tenor voice and a flare for performance, he participated in the cultural opportunities afforded him in Salt Lake City, including singing with the Tabernacle Choir and performing with the Salt Lake Dramatic Association.

Six years after the Teasdales arrived in the Valley, leaders of the Church, recognizing George's talent and education, appointed him to manage the tithing office. A year later, in 1868, he was called to join apostle Albert Carrington and Jesse N. Smith on another full-time mission to the land of his birth. In England he was assigned to the post of assistant editor of the *Millennial Star*. At the conclusion of this mission in 1869, he returned to the United States but remained in New York for a season, assisting with the Church's immigration efforts there. When Elder Teasdale finally reached Utah, he worked for ZCMI, helping to build it up to a business with many hundreds of thousands of dollars of revenue per year. His next mission call came in 1875. He was sent to the southern states, where he labored in Tennessee, Virginia, and North Carolina. At the end of this mission, he returned to Utah and became involved in the mercantile trade again and many other businesses and civic pursuits, including two years of service in the Utah Legislature from 1880 to 1882. Though very successful in all of these undertakings, he had still not come to the end of his numerous missions. After President Taylor received the revelation calling him to the apostleship in 1882, Elder Teasdale was sent on three more missions. First to the Indian Territory, then to Mexico, and finally once again to England, where he served as president of the European Mission for four years.[5]

He always sought inspiration in his callings and had great faith in the Lord and his servants. On one occasion, a recently called missionary from Denmark came to President Teasdale's office to question why he had been called to serve in Germany when he spoke Danish and could be so much more effective preaching in his native tongue. President Teasdale did not try to second guess the calling but had faith that it was from the Lord. He counseled the young man to simply accept his call and depart for his mission. Shortly after this elder's arrival in his field of labor, Schleswig-Holstien, Germany, the missionary found a large number of Scandinavians who had come to that area to build a canal. He preached the gospel to them in Danish, converting many.[6]

Elder Teasdale was loved and respected wherever he served. He traveled widely, helping to organize stakes and wards throughout Utah until his death on 9 June 1907. At the time of his death, the *Deseret Evening News* praised his character and his labors: "[Elder Teasdale] has been singularly blessed in his labors in the ministry, at home and abroad. [He had] a conspicuous type of spirituality that our religion produces. This was in fact his leading trait of character. Amid the toil and privations entailed by the struggle for material existence in pioneer Utah and pioneer Mexico, he still retained the sweetness of his spirituality, and that was indeed of a high order." The eulogy also pointed out that he was not one to delve into obscure or controversial doctrines, but liked to preach the simple truth of the Atonement of Jesus Christ: "The main thing with him was the work of the Redeemer of the world, and how it can touch the conduct of men. The Lord gave him light to see it."[7] George Teasdale was seventy-five years old when he died. He certainly led a long and useful life of service to the cause he had embraced and espoused so ardently as a courageous, inquisitive upholstery shop boy so long ago in his native England.

Notes

1. James R. Clark, *Messages of the First Presidency of the Church of Jesus Christ of Latter-day Saints 1833–1964* (Salt Lake City: Bookcraft, 1965), 2:348.
2. Matthias F. Cowley, *Prophets and Patriarchs* (Chattanooga, TN: Ben E. Rich, 1902), 262.
3. Ibid., 264.
4. Ibid., 265.
5. Ibid., 266.
6. Ibid., 267–68.
7. *Deseret Evening News*, 9 Jun. 1907; in Andrew Jenson, *Latter-day Saint Biographical Encyclopedia* (Salt Lake City: Andrew Jenson History Company, 1920), 3:790.

CHARLES WILLIAM PENROSE

Birth: 4 February 1832, London, Surrey County, England
Baptism: 14 May 1850
Emigration: 1861
Ordination to the Quorum of the Twelve: 7 July 1904
Ordination as Second Counselor to President Joseph F. Smith: 7 December 1911
Ordination as First Counselor to President Heber J. Grant: 10 March 1921
Death: 15 May 1925 (age 93), Salt Lake City, Utah

Unlike most nineteenth-century British converts, Charles William Penrose was not born into poverty. His father, Richard, who owned a tin mine, died while Charles was still a child.[1] His mother, Matilda Sims, was a well-educated and cultured woman and "took great pride in her only son."[2] Active in the Baptist Church, she taught him to memorize long passages of scriptures at age four. He was so precocious that his recitations became a matter of entertainment at social gatherings for his mother's fellow church members. Before his death, Charles's father sometimes took him to London pubs, where the little boy read difficult daily newspaper articles aloud for the amusement of the clientele.[3]

Charles first heard of the Mormon Church as a young boy when he was studying American Indians and came across a story about Joseph Smith telling Indians where they had come from. For some reason, the idea fascinated him, and he decided to look into the origin of the Book of Mormon and started investigating the Church. He had arrived at the conclusion several years earlier that there could be only one true church, which must be the same as the New Testament church. Upon discovering the restored gospel, he declared that The Church of Jesus Christ of Latter-day Saints was "a perfect reproduction of the church established by Jesus Christ," and that it had "the same Divine authority . . . the same promises and the same powers."[4] It was no great surprise that his widowed Baptist mother opposed his joining the strange new sect. She and his sisters never accepted any part of George's new religion, but in later years, as he served missions in England, he visited them and even gave his sister away in marriage.

He joined the Church at age eighteen. Six months later he was called to go on a mission. At that time, the elders went without purse or scrip, a real hardship for a young man who had never experienced a day of poverty in his life. One writer paints the scene in these words: "After having been accustomed to the luxuries of life, it indeed took a brave heart and great faith to leave it all and go out as a missionary without purse or scrip to find shelter and food the best he could, depending entirely upon the Lord."[5]

Remarkably, this mission lasted ten years. Every year he hoped he would be released from his duties and be allowed to immigrate to Zion as had so many of the Saints he baptized. But that was not to be. He stayed on and on, and because in later years he served three more missions, he probably served more years as a missionary than any other member of the Church—a total of seventeen years, all of them in England. About halfway through this first mission, in 1854, Charles met and subsequently married Lucetta Stratford. They began immediately to dream of their voyage to the beautiful mountains of Deseret.

Still an active proselytizing missionary, Elder Penrose was walking one day, his feet bleeding, on a dusty road near Essex. He began to contemplate the Zion he so longed to reach. Being very literary-minded, and having written up to this point a number of songs and poems, words about Zion began to form in his mind. He then composed the beautiful lyrics to the still-popular hymn "O Ye Mountains High," setting it to a familiar English tune. He is also the author of "School Thy Feelings, O My Brother." Two other hymns he authored also appear in our current hymn book, "Up Awake, Ye Defenders of Zion" and "God of Our Fathers, We Come Unto Thee." Besides being an accomplished writer, he was a "gifted and powerful speaker" and also possessed a winning sense of humor, which he frequently employed over the pulpit.[6]

In 1861, he was finally released from his mission. He and his wife and children made the voyage to Utah, where they settled in Farmington. Charles, though totally unaccustomed to any kind of physical labor, began farming, hauling firewood, and teaching school in the winter months to make their living as best he could. After only three years, he was again called to go on a mission. He left his first wife, Lucetta; his second wife, Louisa; and his children behind and traveled back to England, where he was assigned to labor in Manchester. During this mission he began writing essays and articles for the *Millennial Star*. Throughout his life he was a prolific writer. In fact, upon his return from this mission, newspaper editing and managing became his lifetime career. In 1870, at the request of apostle Franklin D. Richards, the Penrose family moved to Ogden, where Charles was employed as editor of the *Daily Junction*.

In 1886 he was called on yet another mission to England, his third. The circumstances of the call were somewhat unusual, for he had initially been called to accompany apostle Franklin D. Richards to the East to help in the campaign for statehood. Church leaders, seeing the danger Elder Penrose was in of being arrested for polygamy, quickly called him on another mission to England, and he left directly from the eastern states without even getting to say good-bye to his wives and children. Fortunately for his family, this mission lasted only one year. Upon his return to Utah, he became managing editor of the *Deseret News*, forcefully and eloquently defending the Church and proclaiming the truth through this medium whenever he could. He also wrote a famous series of tracts for missionary work called "Rays of Living Light" for which he became well known.[7]

In 1904, at the age of seventy-two, Elder Penrose was called to serve in the Quorum of the Twelve apostles. Almost immediately he received his fourth mission call—once again to England, where he replaced his fellow apostle, Heber J. Grant, as president of the European Mission. In this capacity, he wrote numerous editorials for the *Millennial Star*, answering many harsh criticisms of the Church and wielding a powerful pen for the cause of Mormonism throughout the British Isles. From 1911 until his death in 1925 he served in the First Presidency as a counselor, first to Joseph F. Smith and subsequently to Heber J. Grant. At the occasion of his ninetieth birthday, the *Improvement Era* carried this tribute: "He is one of the truly great men of this day and generation—one of the few leaders in the realm of genius and intelligence, of whom men and woman yet unborn will say . . . 'There were giants in the earth in those days.' "[8]

Notes

1. "Charles W. Penrose," *Improvement Era*, 1912, 341.
2. Kenneth W. Godfrey, "Charles W. Penrose: The English Mission Years," *BYU Studies* 27 (Winter 1987): 114.
3. Annie Lynch, "Builders of the West: Charles W. Penrose," *New West Magazine* (1925): 35; in Godfrey, *BYU Studies*, 114.
4. Charles W. Penrose, *Poems*, comp. Ruth McQuarrie Penrose (Salt Lake City: Deseret News Press, 1950), 7; in Godfrey, *BYU Studies*,114.
5. Kate B. Carter, *Heart Throbs of the West* (Salt Lake City: Daughters of the Utah Pioneers, 1948), 3:81.
6. Godfrey, *BYU Studies*, 117–18.
7. Lawrence R. Flake, *Prophets and Apostles of the Last Dispensation* (Provo, UT: BYU Religious Studies Center, 2001), 196.
8. "Ninetieth Anniversary of Pres. Charles W. Penrose," *Improvement Era*, Feb. 1922, 358.

GEORGE REYNOLDS

Birth: 1 January 1842, Marylebone, London, England
Baptism: 4 May 1856
Emigration: 1865
Ordination to First Quorum of the Seventy: 5 April
  1890
Death: 9 August 1909 (age 67), Salt Lake City, Utah

Seven-year-old George Reynolds was such a precocious child that when he heard some of the workers in his father's London tailor shop talking about a new American religion, he knew what they meant when they referred to the Urim and Thummim, having learned of this obscure concept in the Bible. This was the first time he had heard of Mormonism and, though curious, he was unable to learn very much more until he was nine, when Sarah White, a servant girl in his maternal grandmother's house, took him to a meeting of the small Paddington Branch of the Church. From the first, he believed the gospel and asked to be baptized. The elders, however, refused to perform the ordinance without his parents' approval. His father and mother would not consent to his joining the unpopular sect and forbade him to attend the meetings.[1]

Hoping he would forget his strange notions about joining Mormonism, his parents sent him away to school, including a year in France, where he suffered greatly from homesickness, physical illness, and the frustration of not being able to speak the foreign language. He was only twelve but did manage to learn French, master the basics of six other languages, and establish a strong background in classical literature.[2] This formal schooling served as a foundation for a lifetime of self-education.

Secretly, the heart-sick boy maintained his contact with the Church and began an intense study of the gospel. When he read about the Savior's Second Coming, he was worried that it might occur before he was able to become an official member of the Lord's kingdom. And so, at the age of fourteen, he went to a branch of the Church where he was unknown and entered the waters of baptism. He was confirmed a member of the Church and given the gift of the Holy Ghost by the branch president, who would later emigrate to America and become an apostle, Elder George Teasdale.[3]

After his baptism, he was encouraged along with other members of the Church to be a street preacher, a painful task for him as he was naturally reserved and shy. But he persisted in teaching the gospel he loved on the streets of London for five years. During this time he was apprenticed as a cashier, a clerk, and a bookkeeper but did not take to any of these occupations. His true passion was the gospel, and so in 1861, he was more than willing to leave his work and accept a mission call to serve in the British Mission, headquartered in London.

At that time, apostle George Q. Cannon was serving in the presidency of the mission; the two became friends for life and cohorts in some of the most trying events of Church history. After two years of service in the British Mission, President Cannon called George to serve as the secretary of the European Mission with its headquarters in Liverpool, where he labored diligently, especially with the emigration efforts. Here he met his future wife Mary Ann Tuddenham.[4] He remained in his post until his own immigration to Zion in 1865.

Immediately upon his arrival in Utah, George Reynolds began working for the Church, first in the tithing office, and then in the office of the president under Brigham Young's employ. Except for another mission to Great Britain from May of 1871 to July of 1872, he remained in the Salt Lake Valley, holding various positions and fulfilling assignments under the direction of the First Presidency for the rest of his life. In addition to his duties as secretary to Brigham Young, he served as a regent of the University of Deseret; as an associate editor of the *Deseret News* and the *Juvenile Instructor*; as a director of ZCMI, Zion's Saving Bank, and Deseret Telegraph Line; and as a member of the American Association for the Advancement of Science.

On 3 August 1874, he entered into polygamy. When the leaders of the Church decided to test the constitutionality of an 1862 congressional law against polygamy, the Brethren, chiefly his former mission president, George Q. Cannon, selected George Reynolds to give himself up voluntarily to government officials to be tried under the law as a test case. His trial resulted in a conviction, which resulted in his being sentenced to prison. First incarcerated in Nebraska, he was later moved to the Utah Territorial Penitentiary. He made the best of his painful detention by starting a school for the inmates and working on his writing projects, chief among which was his most ambitions work, *A Complete Concordance to the Book of Mormon*, which was a widely circulated and invaluable aid in studying the scriptures until the age of computers came along and rendered it unnecessary. Because of his natural brilliance and meticulous scholarship, he was considered the Church's leading authority on the Book of Mormon, the House of Israel, and other subjects.[5]

George was released from his prison term in January of 1881 and was subsequently appointed as secretary to President John Taylor. But problems with plural marriage continued to ravage the Church for yet another decade. During these troubled years, George married a third wife, and his entire family suffered as he (and even the wives) hid from authorities to evade arrest.[6] Upon President Taylor's death in 1887, George was kept on without hesitation as secretary to the Twelve and subsequently to President Woodruff. In April 1890, he was called to be a General Authority as one of the First Presidents of the Seventy.

As the Church's perils slowly began to subside after the Manifesto of October 1890, George Reynolds continued his church service, his writing and scholarly pursuits, and his labors editing the *Juvenile Instructor*. He served as assistant general superintendent of the Sunday School for eight years and as secretary to the Missionary Committee until he was no longer able to work. He died in 1909, leaving a noble family consisting of three wives and thirty-two children. Well known as he was throughout the Church, his death was mourned by "thousands who have been honored in personal acquaintance with Brother Reynolds, and [by] many thousands more who have known him through his work alone."[7]

Notes

1. Andrew Jenson, *LDS Biographical Encyclopedia* (Salt Lake City: Andrew Jenson History Company, 1901), 1:206-07.
2. George Reynolds, "Journal of George Reynolds," 6 Jun. 1885, 1:3; in Grant R. Hardy, "George Reynolds: The Early Years" (master's thesis, Brigham Young University, May 1972), 10.
3. Jenson, *Biographical Encyclopedia*, 207.
4. Bruce A. Van Orden, *Prisoner for Conscience' Sake* (Salt Lake City: Deseret Book, 1992), 29–30.
5. Van Orden, *Prisoner*, 137.
6. Ibid., 148–49.
7. "Elder George Reynolds," *Juvenile Instructor* 44 (1 Sept. 1909): 355; in Van Orden, *Prisoner*, 210.

BRIGHAM HENRY ROBERTS

Birth: 13 March 1857, Warrington, Lancashire, England
Baptism: 1866
Emigration: 1866
Ordination as First Quorum of the Seventy: 7 October 1888
Death: 27 September 1933 (age 76), Salt Lake City, Utah

At 3:00 a.m. Ann Roberts awoke, dressed, and stole quietly out into the darkness from her house in Warrington, England. She met with a group of Mormon Saints on the seashore and was baptized a member of The Church of Jesus Christ of Latter-day Saints. The secrecy surrounding the baptism was necessary because Ann's husband, Benjamin, had a strong aversion to her new and greatly misunderstood religion. Though she was back in bed before he arose, he soon discovered her secret and announced, "Ann, I believe thee's been dipped!"[1]

It is hard to imagine what sentiments Ann must have felt as she left England eleven years later to immigrate to Utah, leaving behind, out of necessity, two of her beloved children. Brigham, then five years of age, and his twelve-year-old sister, Mary, were entrusted to the care of separate families while their mother took two little babies on the long and perilous journey. One of them died en route. Ann hoped to establish herself in the valley of the Great Salt Lake and then send for Brigham and Mary. Her husband had joined the Church reluctantly but had soon become inactive and irresponsible, gambling and drinking heavily, and so the couple separated.[2]

For four long years, little Henry, as Brigham was known at the time, remained motherless in England. The people with whom he stayed did not take good care of him, and he was allowed to wander the streets, poverty-stricken and unshepherded. Finally the day came when he and his sister, through the help of the Perpetual Emigration Fund, were able to sail to America with seven hundred other Saints aboard the *John Bright*. Nine-year-old Brigham walked barefooted the last four hundred miles of the journey to the Salt Lake Valley across the plains and mountains, arriving in 1866. At last he was reunited with his mother, who lived in a little one-room cabin in Bountiful. Here he obtained some sporadic elementary schooling, worked in the silver mines, and was apprenticed for three years to a blacksmith, the trade that had been his father's in England.[3]

At the age of eighteen, the once totally illiterate boy became an avid reader and sought higher education, graduating at the top of his class from the Utah University Normal School. He married Sarah Louisa Smith and worked as a teacher and part-time blacksmith until his first mission in 1880. Brigham was called to Iowa and Nebraska and then transferred to the southern states. At the end of this mission, he was asked to remain as acting mission president, though he was only twenty-six. This assignment lasted three more years.

Obeying the counsel of the Brethren, Brother Roberts entered into the covenant of plural marriage, becoming the husband of three wives and the father of fifteen children. In 1886 he was arrested for the practice. On the advice of the Church leaders, he forfeited his thousand-dollar bail bond and traveled to England on a mission, where he edited the *Millennial Star.* Upon his return to the Valley, he took up a career in journalism, becoming the editor of the *Salt Lake Herald.* Brother Roberts contributed numerous works to Church literature, most notable of which was his indispensable *Comprehensive History of the Church*, comprising six volumes and over four thousand pages. One writer commented on this truly remarkable achievement in these words: "Elder Roberts does not permit this work to fall to the level of the commonplace. This is much more than a history—more than a reciting and recording of events. . . . Elder Roberts set forth the truths of God to reflect the beauty and strength inherent in them. . . . Is this the work of a historian? Nay, this is the labor of one inspired of God."[4]

During his life, Brother Roberts authored thirty books and more than a thousand articles, pamphlets, and printed talks, becoming by far the most prolific writer in the Church. Called as a member of the First Council of the Seventy at age thirty-one, he was a vigorous missionary and defender of the faith. From 1923 to 1927 he was president of the Eastern States Mission. Much of his life was inextricably connected with the Utah political scene. He entered into the issues of the day with gusto: "He had a bold and inventive mind which naturally led to unsparing criticism. . . . At times he was dangerously impulsive with his words, and had frequently to suffer for his impulsiveness."[5] He bitterly opposed women's suffrage and even participated in a fiery debate on the subject with a brilliant opponent, Elder Orson F. Whitney. Ironically, within four years, in 1900, the women's votes which he had so strongly opposed helped elect him to Congress.

When he arrived in Washington, he was greeted with a petition that had been circulated throughout the United States by sectarian ministers asking that Congress deny him a seat because of his belief in polygamy. The petition contained seven million names, the longest ever collected in the United States up to that time. In spite of his dynamic and eloquent defense, he was refused his seat.

When defending the beliefs of the Church against the onslaught that beset its first century of existence, he engaged in the battle with "that full measure of flame and fire of his surging spirit sustaining him throughout the conflict, never asking for quarter, but withal as generous as a knight in a tournament. When repelling an attack launched against his faith or his people he wield[ed] the rapier of defense 'as though the strength of twenty men were in his arms.' He [was] truly a formidable champion."[6]

It would be hard to overstate the impact of this brilliant man's life and ministry on the church he loved. In the areas of defending the truth, expanding doctrine orally and in print, recording history, promoting missionary work, and interfacing with the political turmoil of his time, he had few if any peers. Elder Roberts died in 1933 at the age of seventy-six.

In light of the sad period of neglect that Brigham suffered as a child in England, the heights of brilliance and forcefulness to which he ascended were truly dramatic. His one-time opponent, Orson F. Whitney, wrote, "A man of courage, full of energy and vitality, he has risen by sheer force of innate ability, coupled with hard and honest toil, from the humblest walks of life to positions of honor and eminence."[7]

Notes

1. Robert H. Malan, *B. H. Roberts: A Biography* (Salt Lake City: Deseret Book, 1966), 3.
2. Ibid., 4.
3. Ibid., 17.
4. T. Pauly, "Brigham H. Roberts—A Tribute," *Improvement Era*, Nov. 1933, 783.
5. Levi Edgar Young, "President Brigham H. Roberts," *Improvement Era*, Dec. 1933, 838.
6. Pauly, *Improvement Era*, 783.
7. Orson F. Whitney, *History of Utah* (Salt Lake City: George Q. Cannon, & Sons, 1892), 4:431.

JAMES EDWARD TALMAGE

Birth: 21 September 1862, Hungerford, Berkshire County, England

Baptism: 15 June 1873

Emigration: 1876

Ordination to the Quorum of the Twelve: 8 December 1911

Death: 27 July 1933 (age 70), Salt Lake City, Utah

Although baptized in the same manner and by the same authority as the Savior, James E. Talmage's baptism was accompanied by the extreme opposite response from beyond the veil. Whereas at Jesus' baptism "a voice from heaven was heard" (Matthew 3:17), at James Talmage's baptism, the voice seems to have come from the depths of hell.

In the small town of Eddington, England, several members of the Church gathered on the banks of the Kennet River in the darkness of a summer night. The year was 1873, and two of the people present were James E. Talmage, a boy of eleven, and his father, James, the president of the local branch of the Church. When young James was stricken earlier that year with an inexplicable illness, his father felt that an unnecessary delay in the boy's baptism might be the reason for the misfortune. And so, on this warm evening, they stole out quietly near midnight, to avoid the hostile eyes of their anti-Mormon neighbors. Before they could enter the water, they were interrupted. Brother Talmage recalled, "We were veritably horror-stricken by a combined shriek, yell, scream, howl. . . . It seemed to be a combination of every fiendish ejaculation we could conceive of. I remember how I trembled at the awful manifestation. . . . Father, who was also trembling . . . then asked me if I was too frightened to be baptized; I was too much terrified to speak, so I answered by stepping into the water."[1]

The Talmages were never able to discover any natural cause for this blood-curdling noise, nor did anyone else in the community report hearing it, though it was loud enough to have carried a great distance. In analyzing Elder Talmage's life and contemplating the massive influence he had for good, one could only speculate that his baptism might well have brought forth such an outcry from the adversary himself.

Three years later, when James was fourteen, the Talmages immigrated to Utah, settling in Provo, a fortunate location for the boy, who was able to enter Brigham Young Academy under the inspiring tutelage of Karl G. Maeser. Brother Maeser recognized immediately the genius that was to set James E. Talmage in the top ranks of education, science, and theology. James began teaching at Brigham Young Academy at the early age of sixteen for a mere three dollars per week. He was soon offered a much more remunerative position with the Provo city schools, but upon counseling with the Lord in sincere prayer, as was his custom, he felt impressed to remain at the Academy.

When he did leave, it was to seek further learning. While some well-meaning friends warned him against going east to obtain what they feared might he a faith-destroying higher education, President John Taylor, from whom James received counsel during a three-hour session, not only encouraged him to go, but, Elder Talmage reported, "To my grateful surprise, laid his hands on my head and blessed me for the undertaking. The blessing thus pronounced has been realized in both spirit and letter."[2]

James obtained many degrees and scholastic honors, including a bachelor's and a doctorate from Lehigh University in Pennsylvania and a degree from Illinois Wesleyan University in 1896. He also studied for a year at Johns Hopkins University in Baltimore. Brother Talmage was the recipient of several honorary doctorates and was a member of numerous prestigious international scholastic societies. He later became the president of two institutions of higher learning, LDS College in Salt Lake City and the University of Utah.

Eventually leaving his education career behind in favor of becoming a geological engineer and mining consultant, Dr. Talmage utilized the practical aspects of his chosen scientific field. However, this career was short lived because in 1911 he was called to the Quorum of the Twelve. While serving in this office, he continued to receive many lucrative offers in the field of science but gladly turned them down to remain in full-time service to the Lord. That service included a four-year assignment as president of the European Mission, which included his homeland of Britain.

Besides a strong testimony and a brilliant mind, Elder Talmage had another great gift—marvelous fluency and remarkable precision in his mastery of the English language. He wrote numerous scientific and religious works, but his two monumental theological masterpieces, *Articles of Faith* and *Jesus the Christ*, are his greatest legacy to members of the Church. He could easily have become wealthy on the profits from these very popular volumes, but typical of Elder Talmage's generosity, he endowed the Church with the royalties.

At the time of his death on 27 July 1933 at the age of seventy, a beloved fellow apostle, Melvin J. Ballard, noted that while Elder Talmage did not acquire much of this world's goods, he retained in death his real treasures: "He takes with him the things that are worthwhile—a marvelous knowledge, his faith, his well-trained mind, and above all his right to the holy apostleship which he will never forfeit, having honored that calling in this life."[3]

Notes
1. James E. Talmage, "An Unusual Accompaniment to a Baptism," *Improvement Era*, Jun. 1922, 675.
2. Bryant S. Hinckley, "James E. Talmage," *Improvement Era*, July 1932, 524.
3. Melvin J. Ballard, "Dr. James E. Talmage," *Improvement Era*, Sept. 1933, 648; see also John R. Talmage, *The Talmage Story: Life of James E. Talmage—Educator, Scientist, Apostle* (Salt Lake City: Bookcraft, 1972).

JOHN WELLS

Birth: 16 September 1864, Carlton, Nottingham, England

Baptism: 12 August 1882

Emigration: 1889

Ordination as Second Counselor to Presiding Bishop Charles Wilson Nibley: 18 July 1918

Ordination as Second Counselor to Presiding Bishop Sylvester Quayle Cannon: 6 October 1925

Death: 18 April 1941 (age 76), Salt Lake City, Utah

A cheerful English teenager named Arthur Winters had found great joy in the message of Mormonism. Anxious to share that joy, he approached one of his friends, John Wells, who lived near his Nottingham home. The prevailing anti-Mormon attitude of the time had strongly prejudiced John against the Church, and he recoiled at the invitation to learn more about this strange American religion. Although their friendship was strained over the incident, Arthur persisted. John was an extremely intelligent young man, and his friend knew that if he would just give Mormonism a fair hearing, he too would be converted.

An example of his intellect is seen in an incident that took place when John was only ten years old. "At that time the schoolmaster prepared him for an examination for a scholarship. The night before the test, the schoolmaster came to the house to tell him that he had neglected to have him memorize one hundred and twelve lines of the "Lady of the Lake." He had it memorized by morning and was awarded the scholarship."[1]

Arthur's next attempt to interest his friend in the Church was to hide a copy of the Book of Mormon in his bag. When John discovered it, he threw the book down with disgust.

> As he did so, however, he says he heard a voice saying distinctly, "Read the book!". . . Obediently, he picked up the volume once more, with exactly the same result, and again he threw it down in disgust. Thereupon the same voice spoke a second time, "Read the book!" A third time he took up the volume. But instead of beginning with the first page, as he had done the other two times, he opened it at random to one of the last pages. And this is what his eyes fell upon:
>
> *And when ye shall receive these things, I would exhort you that ye would ask God, the Eternal Father, in the name of Christ, if these things are not true; and if ye shall ask with a sincere heart, with real intent, having faith in Christ, he will manifest the truth of it unto you, by the power of the Holy Ghost* [Moroni 10:4]. . . .
>
> He read the Book from cover to cover.[2]

This touching invitation humbled him. He prayed about the book "with real intent" and was soon baptized.

Serving with his friend Arthur as a member of the Aaronic Priesthood, John's talents for organization and leadership were quickly recognized by local Church leaders, and three years later, in 1885, he was called to serve as president of the Nottingham Branch.

The following year he married Almena Thorpe, and they, like many English Saints, dreamed of going to Zion. In 1889 their dream came true—they and their baby sailed for America on the steamship *Wisconsin*, finally arriving in the Salt Lake Valley on July 11. After a few months of employment in the ZCMI shoe factory, Elder Wells was hired as messenger and general office boy by the presiding bishop of the Church, William B. Preston. Because of John's industry and aptitude, he was soon promoted to chief clerk. For twenty years he gave his best to the important work of the presiding bishop's office.

In July 1918 Bishop Charles W. Nibley selected Elder Wells as second counselor in the presiding bishopric, a position he held for another twenty years. Bishop Wells applied his organizational acumen to the problems of a growing church and made significant improvements in the tithing and record keeping systems. So valuable was his service that when Sylvester Q. Cannon became the presiding bishop in 1925, he asked Bishop Wells to continue as his second counselor. At the passing of Bishop Cannon in 1938, John Wells, now seventy-four, was released from his duties.

A few weeks before his own death on 18 April 1941, Bishop Wells spoke at the funeral of Arthur Winters and expressed gratitude to his boyhood friend who had led him, sixty years earlier in England, to what he counted his greatest treasure—membership in The Church of Jesus Christ of Latter-day Saints.[3]

Notes

1. Margaret Newman Wells and Clarice Wells Crook, "Bishop John Wells: His Life and Labors," quarto, BYU Special Collections, 30 Apr. 1973, 1.
2. John Henry Evans, "Conversions Through the Book of Mormon: IV in England," *Instructor* (Jan. 1944): 57.
3. See Lawrence R. Flake, *Mighty Men of Zion: General Authorities of the Last Dispensation* (Salt Lake City: Karl D. Butler, 1974), 516.

JOHN LONGDEN

Birth: 4 November 1898, Oldham, Lancashire, England
Baptism: 1906
Emigration: unknown
Ordination as Assistant to the Quorum of the Twelve: 6 October 1951
Death: 30 August 1969 (age 70), Salt Lake City, Utah

In September of 1909, shortly before his family emigrated from their home in England to Salt Lake City, ten-year-old John Longden was introduced by his father to an important Church leader, apostle Charles W. Penrose. Elder Penrose was at the time president of the British Mission with its headquarters in Liverpool, and upon his return to Salt Lake City, he would become a member of the First Presidency. That same year that John met him, President Penrose dedicated "a little corrugated, galvanized meetinghouse in Oldham, Lancashire, [the town] where [Longden] was born."[1] Who could have predicted that fifty-six years later, John Longden, now a General Authority himself, would return to England at the behest of President David O. McKay to dedicate a beautiful new chapel in that very place. In a conference address a few months later, Elder Longden said, "My, what a contrast from the little galvanized building in which I used to go to Sunday School and sacrament meeting and all the other services that were held at that time. . . . Fifty-six years ago! It seems like yesterday! How time flies!"[2]

In Utah, John Longden was educated at the Latter-day Saint High School, LDS Business College, and the University of Utah. Possessed of a natural talent for music and drama, he studied voice, acting, and violin and joined two different stock companies, performing throughout Utah and Idaho.

In 1924, after fulfilling a mission to the central states, he married Frances LaRue Carr in the Salt Lake Temple. The Longdens were the parents of three daughters. Their firstborn, Helen Margaret, died when she was three years old. Of this experience, Elder Longden expressed these courageous sentiments just a few months before his own death: "I have seen my own child laid away . . . and numerous other things have happened to me which have certainly made me sure of the true values in life, so I do feel that if given the opportunity, I could help bring satisfaction, solace, and perhaps a little happiness to the lives of others."[3]

Professionally Elder Longden started out in the insurance field and later entered the area of electrical supply. In this business he became the manager of Western Electrical Supply and later of National Electric Products Corporation.

His record of service in the Church shows his great devotion. He served as bishop of the Salt Lake City Nineteenth Ward, was on the high council of the Salt Lake and Highland stakes for a total of seventeen years, became a member of the Church's General Welfare Committee in 1950, and was called as an assistant to the Twelve in 1951.

Elder Longden used his musical talent to inspire and uplift members of the Church. Often when he had a speaking assignment, he also could be persuaded to sing,[4] bearing testimony in his beautiful voice with a selection such as his favorite hymn, "I Know that My Redeemer Lives." With his many talents and all of his resources, he served valiantly as a General Authority until his death in August 1969 at the age of seventy. At the time of his passing, the First Presidency issued a statement regarding their "beloved associate," Elder John Longden: "His was a life of devoted, faithful and unselfish service. He used his many talents for the blessing of his church and community, and will be greatly missed by his many friends, associates and loved ones. We acknowledge the sterling qualities of his leadership and dedication in the service of The Master."[5]

Notes
1. John Longden, Conference Report, 6 April 1966, 37–38.
2. *Church News*, September 6, 1969, 4.
3. Ibid.
4. Ibid.

DEREK A. CUTHBERT

Birth: 5 October 1926, Nottingham, Derbyshire, England
Baptism: 27 January 1951
Emigration: 1978
Ordination to the First Quorum of the Seventy: 1 April 1978
Death: 7 April 1991 (age 64), Salt Lake City, Utah

On a sultry August day in 1950, three Mormon missionaries were going door to door in a neighborhood of Nottingham England. They were planning to close down the work in that area but decided to knock on one last door. To their surprise and joy, the lady of the house invited them in. Muriel Cuthbert knew nothing about The Church of Jesus Christ of Latter-day Saints but had heard that a distant cousin of hers was a "Mormon" and was serving a mission somewhere in England. She later discovered that her great-great-grandmother and her grandmother had also joined the Church, but Mormonism had not made it down the family tree to her.[1] Muriel Cuthbert and her husband Derek had been active members of the Church of England all of their lives as had most of their progenitors for centuries before them. They had no interest in changing denominations. During a subsequent visit by the missionaries, Derek told them that he and his wife "were interested in their message but would never join the Church."[2] One of the elders wrote in his journal that night that the Cuthberts would be baptized within six months.

The prophecy came to pass five months later in January of 1951. Recounting their conversion experience to the students of Brigham Young University in a campus devotional three decades later, Elder Cuthbert recalled, "Mormon missionaries were led—and I repeat were led—to our door. As a matter of fact, the Lord sent three missionaries to our door. (He knew it might be tough.) Furthermore, my wife informed me they all had the same first name—Elmer Jones, Elmer Cordingly, and Elmer Seastrand!"[3]

Being a Mormon in England at that time was not easy, and the young couple (he was only twenty-three) experienced a lot of prejudice from friends and neighbors. But as time went on, most of their associates came to accept and even admire them and their growing family, which would eventually consist of six daughters and four sons. Brother Cuthbert remembers, "Before we were baptized, we vowed that the Church would be our life. We have never had one doubt, nor one regret."[4]

Derek was a native of Nottingham, born there October 6, 1926, the second son of Harry Cuthbert and Hilda May Freck. His mother was a devout member of the Church of England and taught her sons to read the Bible and to pray. Derek sang in the choir, attended services, and was confirmed in August of 1938 at the age of twelve. Coincidentally, his future wife, Muriel Olive Mason, was confirmed on the same day and the two formed a fast friendship. England at that time was deeply affected by the looming threats of war. Sadly, that same year, Derek's mother had a nervous breakdown from which she never fully recovered. "Derek felt that his mother's illness had a greater personal effect on his early teenage years than did World War II, and forced him to become more independent and mature."[5] The following year, 1939, England was plunged into the war. Three years later, Derek joined the Home Guard at the age of only sixteen, and at eighteen, the Royal Air Force. In 1945 when the war ended, he married his longtime friend and sweetheart, Muriel.

Following his marriage, his tour of duty in the air force included serving for three years in India, Burma, and Hong Kong. Upon his return to England, he graduated with honors in economics and law from the University of Nottingham and launched a career in chemicals, textiles, and plastics.[6] Money was tight when the Cuthberts joined the Church, but they exercised their faith and paid their tithing. Although a friend warned Derek that if he didn't drink and smoke his career would be ruined, he prospered. Because of their spirit and dedication, the newly converted couple was soon put to work by local Church leaders, strengthening the Saints in the land of their birth. It soon became obvious that Elder Cuthbert's extensive Church callings put the family in dire need of owning a car. Because he was only a junior trainee in his company, his colleagues viewed the purchase of a car as a bit premature. But again, the Cuthberts exercised their faith and bought the car. Shortly afterward, Derek was promoted and received just enough of a raise to cover the expenses of the car and of his travels for the Church.[7]

Although tens of thousands of Latter-day Saints had joined the Church in England during the 1800s, more than 80,000 had immigrated to the United States, leaving many of the local congregations weak and struggling.[8] There was only one mission with fourteen districts in all of Britain. Finally, in 1960, the first stake in England was formed in Manchester, and a second stake in London the next year. When a third stake was formed in Leicester a few weeks later, Derek Cuthbert became its president, the first native born Briton to receive that calling in England. Later he was set apart by President Spencer W. Kimball as the president of the Birmingham Stake. Next came a call to serve as a Regional Representative of the Twelve for the British Isles. In 1971 he was serving in this capacity when ninety-five year-old President Joseph Fielding Smith came to England to preside over the first area conference held anywhere in the Church. Brother Cuthbert was appointed conference chairman with responsibility for organizing what was the largest gathering of Saints ever in Great Britain.[9] Elder Cuthbert enjoyed the opportunity of driving President Smith around the area where he (President Smith) had served as a young missionary more than seventy years before. A picture of the two men appeared on the front cover of the *Ensign* magazine the following month.

Four years later in 1975, Elder Cuthbert accepted a call to be the president of the Scotland Edinburgh Mission. On New Year's Day, 1976, President Cuthbert and a number of his missionaries climbed a famous hill in Edinburgh known as "Arthur's Seat." One hundred thirty-six years before, Elder Orson Pratt of the Quorum of the Twelve ascended the same hill for the same reason—to dedicate the city to missionary work. Both men were very specific in their petitions to the Lord. Elder Pratt asked for 200 souls to join the Church. President Cuthbert requested 300 male converts to strengthen the Church there. By the time his mission presidency was completed, almost exactly that number of brethren had been baptized.

In March of 1978, President Cuthbert received a stunning telephone call from President Spencer W. Kimball, inviting him to become a member of the First Quorum of the Seventy. With characteristic humility and dedication, he and his family prepared to move to Salt Lake City. " 'It overwhelmed us,' Elder Cuthbert recalls. 'And it was difficult to leave our native land for America, particularly since we had been teaching the British Saints for twenty-eight years that "non-emigration" was the policy of the Church! But we were glad to serve the Lord in any capacity.' "¹⁰

For the next dozen years, Derek Cuthbert traveled the world as a special witness of the Lord Jesus Christ, serving in area presidencies from Idaho to the Midwest and from Canada to Africa. Perhaps his favorite assignment was being a member of the Europe Area Presidency, which included his beloved native land of England.

Beginning in 1976, Elder Cuthbert began to have some serious health problems. He suffered from numbness in his feet and legs and from diabetes. In 1989 he was diagnosed with an advanced case of cancer that had spread into both of his lungs. Following surgery and extensive chemotherapy, his lungs healed, and he miraculously returned to almost normal. He attributed his recovery to the many members of the Church throughout the world who prayed for him, sent him cards and letters, and made encouraging and loving phone calls. Many fasted for him, including his fellow members of the Quorum of the Seventy. He also received many priesthood blessings from them and from his beloved sons and sons-in-law.¹¹

When President Gordon B. Hinckley stood to give his concluding remarks of the April 1991 General Conference, he announced, "We have just received a telephone call that Elder Derek Cuthbert has just passed away. We have been praying for him. He has served faithfully and diligently and well as a member of the First Quorum of the Seventy."¹² At his funeral a few days later, President Hinckley declared, "I'm grateful for such men as Derek Cuthbert. There's never any question about where they stand. Nobody can question their integrity. No one can question their faith. No one can question their sense of duty. . . . God be thanked for him and his kind!"[13]

Notes

1. Derin Head Rodrigues, *From Every Nation* (Salt Lake City: Deseret Book, 1990), 69-70.
2. Derek A. Cuthbert, *The Second Century: Latter-day Saints in Great Britain*, vol. 1, *1937–1987* (Cambridge, England: Cambridge University Press, 1987), 5.
3. Derek A. Cuthbert, "The Business of Being" (devotional assembly, Brigham Young University, Provo, UT, 19 May 1981); in *New Era*, July 1983, 46.
4. Breck England, "Elder Derek A. Cuthbert: British Leader Is 'At Home' in the Lord's Work," *Ensign*, Sept. 1984, 19.
5. Rodriguez, 67.
6. Breck, 19.
7. Rodriguez, 71-72.
8. *Second Century*, 2.
9. Ibid., iii.
10. Breck, 1.
11. Rodgriguez, 79-80.
12. Derek A. Cuthbert, in Conference Report, April 1991.
13. "News of the Church," *Ensign* May 1991, 103.

KENNETH JOHNSON

Birth: 5 July 1940, Norwich, England
Baptism: 16 August 1959
Emigration: 1990
Ordination to the Second Quorum of the Seventy: 31
*   March 1990*
Ordination to the First Quorum of the Seventy: 3 April
*   1993*

W orld War II imposed many hardships on the people of England. For little Kenneth Johnson, born in Norwich in 1940, it meant not getting to meet his own father until he was five years old. Like most able-bodied Englishmen, Kenneth's father was in the British Army. He was stationed in Italy. Elder Johnson recalls,

> My first recollection of meeting my father occurred when I was five years old. A telegram was delivered to our home. My mother stood with the gold-colored envelope in her hand, making no attempt to open it. I did not realize then as I do now the reason why, and the message it could have contained. Eventually and with great difficulty, she fumbled with the flap of the envelope. This seemed to take a long time. . . . Finally, raising the telegram high above her head, my mother joyfully exclaimed, "Dad's coming home! Dad's coming home!" . . . and with a skipping step, set out in the direction of my grandparents' home, shouting, "Dad's coming home! Dad's coming home!" My brother, following close behind, shouted, "Dad's coming home! Dad's coming home!" I brought up the rear, also shouting, "Dad's coming home! Dad's coming home! Who's Dad?"
>
> The next morning when I awoke, there was a man sitting on the edge of my bed holding a leather soccer ball from Italy. He asked if my brother and I would like to play soccer with him. Cautiously I agreed.[1]

Kenneth drew very close to his father, whom he describes as "a very humble yet brilliant man." He remembers that "he sang in the Methodist choir, but his religion was not in churches."[2] He gratefully acknowledges his "dear parents, who reared [him] in such a way that when the truth came, [he] would recognize it."[3]

The truth came to Kenneth in 1959 when he was nineteen and attended a dance where he met a beautiful girl named Pamela Wilson. The first time he had ever heard of The Church of Jesus Christ of Latter-day Saints was when Pam told him she was a member of it. He recalls, "I was impressed enough with Pam that whatever being a Mormon meant had to be good."⁴ She made it clear from the start that she would never marry unless it was to a member of the Church and in the temple. Pam had grown up in a small, struggling branch of the Church in England, but her parents were strong members, and when she was a little girl they promised her, "One day you will go to the temple"—a fairly bold promise to make in a country where there was no temple at that time. Not surprisingly, Kenneth decided to investigate the gospel. Four months later he was baptized, and three years later he and Pam were married in the new London Temple.⁵

Graduating from Norwich City College and the London Institute of Printing, Kenneth pursued a career in the printing trade, later switching tracks to the insurance business. The young couple was blessed with only one child, a son who was born with serious complications. With characteristic gratitude, Kenneth declared, "We got such a good one the first time, we were not blessed with any more."⁶ Elder Johnson said, "I promised the Lord that if His dews of heaven would distil upon my son and preserve him, I would give my life to fulfill his work of love."⁷ The Lord did distil his blessings, and their son overcame his difficulties and was able to serve a mission, be married in the temple, and follow his father's example of faithful service in the Church.

Elder Johnson fulfilled and continues to fulfill his part of the covenant with the Lord, having served in branch and district presidencies and for ten years as stake president—first in Ipswich and then in Norwich, England. Next he labored as a regional representative until accepting a call to full-time Church service as a member of the Second Quorum of the Seventy. Just three years into that five-year assignment, on 3 April 1993, he was sustained to the First Quorum, where he continues to serve faithfully as he promised the Lord he would.

Notes

1. Kenneth Johnson, "We All Have a Father in Whom We Can Trust," *Ensign*, May 1994, 29.

2. "News of the Church," *Ensign*, May 1990, 105.
3. Ibid.
4. Ibid.
5. Hilary Hendricks and Kenneth Johnson, "Friend to Friend: Keeping Promises," *Friend*, Sept. 2001, 8.
6. Kenneth Johnson, "Who's in Control?" *New Era*, July 1993, 44.
7. Ibid.

CONCLUSION

The lives of these twelve noble Englishmen who became leaders of the Church span a period of two centuries, from John Taylor's birth in 1808 to the Kenneth Johnson's present service as a member of the Seventy.

They have served in all of the General Authority callings, including one that no longer exists, assistant to the Twelve. It is impossible to calculate the amount of good they have accomplished. Collectively, they have baptized hundreds of converts and strengthened literally millions of members of the Church. Most of them have contributed to the great library of faith-promoting literature that Church members hold dear.

Additionally, and perhaps most important, each of these great brethren leaves a noble and ever-expanding posterity, who, inspired by the example of a faithful progenitor, continue to build the restored kingdom. Thanks be to God for these twelve remarkable sons of Britain.

ABOUT THE AUTHOR

Dr. Lawrence R. Flake is a professor of Church history and doctrine at Brigham Young University. He earned his master's degree and doctorate from BYU in religious education and has served as a teacher and an administrator for the Church Educational System for four decades in Utah; New York; Washington, D.C.; and Montana. He has given talks and lectures throughout the United States and has traveled extensively abroad, including a six-month assignment to the BYU Jerusalem Center. Professor Flake has written for various periodicals, journals, and encyclopedias. He is the author of five books, including *Prophets and Apostles of the Last Dispensation*. He has served in many callings in the Church, including regional representative, and as president of the Missouri Independence Mission. He and his wife, Elaine, who has also taught religion classes at BYU, are the parents of eight children.